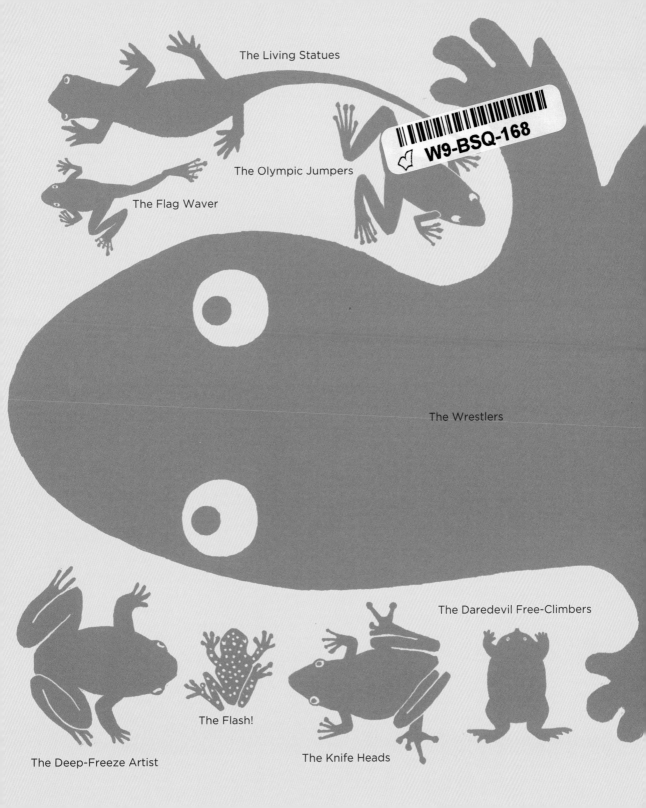

The Living Statues

The Olympic Jumpers

The Flag Waver

The Wrestlers

The Daredevil Free-Climbers

The Deep-Freeze Artist

The Flash!

The Knife Heads

Amphibian
Acrobats

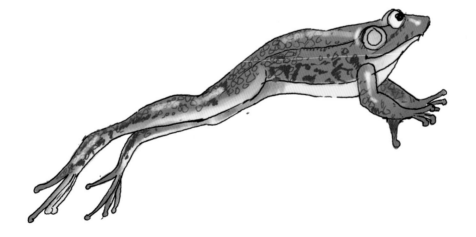

Amphibian Acrobats

Written by **Leslie Bulion**

Illustrated by **Robert Meganck**

PEACHTREE

ATLANTA

For Charlie T.
—L. B.

To the army of frogs that shared the swamp with me:
R1, R3, R4, R5, R6, and R7.
—R2

Published by
Peachtree Publishing Company Inc.
1700 Chattahoochee Avenue
Atlanta, Georgia 30318-2112
www.peachtree-online.com

Text © 2020 by Leslie Bulion
Illustrations © 2020 by Robert Meganck

Edited by Vicky Holifield
Design and composition by Robert Meganck
Art direction by Nicola Simmonds Carmack

The illustrations were rendered digitally.

Printed in August 2019 by Tien Wah Press, Malaysia
10 9 8 7 6 5 4 3 2 1 (hardcover)
10 9 8 7 6 5 4 3 2 1 (trade paperback)
First Edition

HC ISBN: 978-1-68263-098-3
PB ISBN: 978-1-68263-184-3

Library of Congress Cataloging-in-Publication Data

Names: Bulion, Leslie, 1958– author. | Meganck, Robert, illustrator.
Title: Amphibian acrobats / written by Leslie Bulion ; illustrated by Robert Meganck.
Description: First edition. | Atlanta, Georgia : Peachtree Publishing Company Inc., [2020] | Audience: Age 8–12. | Audience: Grade 4 to 6. | Includes bibliographical references.
Identifiers: LCCN 2019019035 | ISBN 9781682630983
Subjects: LCSH: Amphibians—Juvenile literature.
Classification: LCC QL644.2 .B85 2020 | DDC 597.8—dc23 LC record available at *https://lccn.loc.gov/2019019035*

Amphibian Acrobats

We're amphibians! We breathe through our skin,
We drink the same way: we soak water in,
Through skin that is moist-ily marvelous thin—
Come see our amazing show!

Caecilians, salamanders, toads, and frogs,
In leaf litter, treetops, and snugged under logs,
In deserts and forests and swampy wet bogs—
All excellent spots for our show!

We march, burrow, hop, we climb rainforest trees,
We leap, using leaves like a flying trapeze,
We chill to amphib-sicles—*some of us freeze!*
Come see our astonishing show!

We're shape shifters, starting the moment we hatch,
(In water or out) from our jelly-egg batch,
Some can drop tails then regrow them *from scratch*—
All part of our fabulous show!

We gulp little critters—*whap-snap*—with no fuss,
We keep pests in check on our Earth—*that's* a plus,
But when we're still tadpoles or eggs, pests eat *us*—
(Our least favorite act in the show).

So strap on your headlamp to have the best view,
We're here in the spotlight, come see what we do.
Step right up...

    turn the page...

        let us dazzle you through...

Our Amphibian Acrobat show!

Amazing Amphibians

Amphibians—frogs, salamanders, and caecilians (seh-SIH-lee-enz)—are a group of animals with backbones (vertebrates) found on every continent except Antarctica. They are ectothermic (EK-toe-THUR-mik), which means their bodies are warmed and cooled by their surroundings. Most amphibians hatch from soft, jelly-coated eggs into larvae (young forms) that grow and change into adults in the process called metamorphosis (met-uh-MOR-fuh-sis).

Amphibians do most of their breathing and take in nearly all of the water they need through their thin skin. But skin that's thin enough for water to pass *in* also allows water to evaporate *out*. This is why many amphibians live in or near water for at least part of their life cycle.

All adult amphibians are carnivores that gobble many kinds of prey, including flying, aquatic (water-living), and leaf litter critters. But some tasty prey (such as dragonflies and damselflies) begin their lives as aquatic predators that happily munch tadpoles and salamander larvae, circling this food *web* around into a food *loop*.

Ready to meet these showstoppers? *Step right up!*

 Frogs leap, hop, and even glide. All frogs (including the family of frogs we call toads) go through BIG changes as they metamorphose from wriggling tadpoles to jumping adults.

 Salamanders hatch as larvae with three pairs of plumelike gills outside their bodies. Most species lose their gills and develop into four-legged, walking adults.

 Caecilians burrow their legless, worm-shaped bodies into soil and leaf litter. Some are completely aquatic. Many caecilian moms give birth to live young instead of laying eggs.

The Olympic Jumpers

Some Fiji frogs—gold with brown traces,
are leaping, escape-artist aces.
With a twist in midair,
they land backwards and hop
where no frog-hungry snake ever faces.

Fiji Tree Frog

Frogs are built for JUMPING! Their long-boned back legs help them leap away from predators such as snakes, birds, lizards, and small mammals. Takeoff is powered by strong hind-leg muscles that launch their short bodies up with no tail to weigh them down. Swimming frogs use those big muscles to kick away from hungry salamanders, waterbirds, and fish. Frogs have all kinds of athletic, action-packed strategies to keep from becoming froggy snacks.

The nocturnal (active at night) Fiji tree frog (*Cornufer vitiensis*), found only on the South Pacific islands of Fiji, escapes from danger with a surprise aerial twist. Instead of a straight-up leap, this fancy jumper swivels in midair. When it lands, the Fiji tree frog is facing sideways or backwards. Then it hops off in an unexpected direction, befuddling its still-hungry predator: *Hah! Missed me!*

The Skydiver

This tree frog's feet are flappy, yes they are.
They're webbed with skin that's inky black, like tar,
Like night sky with a yellow, frog-toe star.

This largish frog with bright white, bulgy eyes,
Flees any treetop perch where danger lies,
By paragliding with its feet—*it flies!*

Wallace's Flying Frog

Wallace's flying frog (*Rhacophorus nigropalmatus*) uses its sticky toe pads to hold tight to trees high in the rainforests of Southeast Asia, Malaysia, and Indonesia. This excellent climber also has another super-acrobat trick.

With a leap, this nocturnal tree frog splays long, spindly legs and catches air using the black webbing between its yellow fingers and toes. As its legs spread horizontally, this webbing plus skin flaps on the frog's sides help to slow and steer its forward glide. When the flying frog reaches its next leaf or branch, big toe pads on its flappy, floppy feet help stick its landing.

These big, but hard-to-spot, frogs stay in the trees until a sudden downpour signals Wallace's flying frogs to descend to ground level and seek a mate. Mating pairs protect their fertilized eggs with a frothy bubble nest stuck to leaves or branches above a rain pool or large animal wallow. When tadpoles hatch, they'll squirm out and drop in for a swim—*plink, plink, plink!*

The Shape Shifter

Pebble toad, sensing trouble,
tenses, forms a frog-ball, tumbles. Bounces
downhill over brambles. Ricochets off sandstone
rubble. Rolls to rest, unfurls. No wobbles.
Rambles on unhurt, ungobbled.

Venezuelan Pebble Toad

"True toads" are frogs in the family called *Bufonidae* (boo-FAH-nih-day). Most true toads have drier and bumpier skin, shorter hind legs built for hopping, and no teeth. Most also make irritating chemicals in lumpy glands at the back of their head. But some frogs with the word "toad" in their common name aren't members of the family *Bufonidae* at all—even if they share some of these toadlike traits.

The Venezuelan pebble toad (*Oreophrynella nigra*) is a chubby little member of the true toad family. Blackish-gray to match the daytime sandstone mountains in its eastern Venezuela home, this slow-moving toad can make a tricky-quick getaway. If it meets danger (a meal-seeking tarantula, perhaps) the pebble toad tucks its head and legs, tenses its muscles, and rolls away downslope. It bounces and topples down, down, down, coming to rest when safely out of reach. Then the pebble unfolds into a toad and continues on its hoppy way.

The Knife Heads

jabbity stabbity
Bruno's frog, Greening's frog,
cuties, until hidden
skull daggers poke

through their strong skin toxins,
head-butt-injectingly,
venomous frogs can make
predators croak!

Bruno's Casque-Headed Frog and Greening's Frog

Scientists have identified at least 300 poison dart frog species, all found in Central or South America. These brightly colored diurnal (active by day) frogs, and many other frogs worldwide, ooze toxic substances from their skin that are irritating, bad-tasting, or poisonous to eat.

The skins of two frogs from Brazil, Bruno's casque-headed frog (*Aparasphenodon brunoi*) and Greening's frog (*Corythomantis greeningi*) also contain harmful substances. But unlike poison dart frogs that are dangerous *to eat*, these two frogs can inject their toxins through another animal's skin using weapons hidden in their heads! Toxin delivered with a sharp spine or fang is called venom.

When these nocturnal frogs are threatened, bony spines on their skulls poke through their venom-filled skin. This doesn't hurt their own scalps, but a venom-coated, spiky header is no joke for potential predators, many of which seem to know to stay away. By day, Bruno's and Greening's frogs tuck feet-first into hidey-holes. Their weapony helmet-heads act as lids on the holes, keeping moisture in and predators OUT.

The Deep-Freeze Artist

This frogsicle outwits Jack Frost
with frog pipes full of antifreeze.
Though frog-ice solid, all's not lost.
This frogsicle outwits Jack Frost—
heartbeat, breathing stopped—no cost.
Until spring rains wake sleeping trees,
this frogsicle outwits Jack Frost
with frog pipes full of antifreeze!

North American Wood Frog

Warm, moist climates are the perfect home for most frog species. Cold-climate frogs must burrow into soil or pond mud to survive killing frosts.

The only amphibian able to live above the Arctic circle, the widespread North American wood frog (*Lithobates sylvaticus*) has a fancy trick to survive extreme cold. This daytime woods-dweller can make sugary "antifreeze" in its liver. The antifreeze replaces nearly two-thirds of all the water between the cells in the frog's body. A few other frogs make antifreeze, but the wood frog is the champ!

Burrowed in winter soil with its antifreeze on board, the wood frog can freeze solid. It will stop breathing and its heart stops beating for weeks at a time. When temperatures rise, it can take up to 24 hours for a wood frog's body functions to come back online. This freeze-thaw cycle may happen several times during the cold winter months. When nearby vernal pools thaw, wood frogs fully defrost and the loud, daytime *quack-quacking* of their mating swim party begins!

The Flash!

Nobody knows
why this tree frog glows,
from glimmering nose
to gleaming toes.
Camouflage? Messaging?
Neither of those?
No herpetologist knows.

Nobody knows
why this tree frog glows.
By day it may doze
resting still, in repose,
but night is for calling
while striking a pose,
in thin, see-through skin through which
blue-green glow shows.
Who sees this glow?
Nobody knows!

Polka-Dot Tree Frog

Many frogs are masters of camouflage. Drab, mottled patterns on their backs break up their froggy outlines. Skin flaps, bumps, and changeable skin textures help frogs blend in with leaves, pebbles, or moss. Predators such as hungry birds, snakes, or small mammals can miss these hidden meals.

The polka-dot tree frog (*Hypsiboas punctatus*) is a nocturnal frog from South America. Similar to the group known as "glass frogs," this frog has see-through skin that makes it hard to spot when perched on a rainforest leaf. And the polka-dot tree frog has an even flashier trick. Under ultraviolet light (UV, or black light), the frog glows bright greenish blue. Frog scientists have found special molecules in this frog's body and skin that absorb light, then send light out again at longer wavelengths—that's called fluorescence. How does fluorescence help the polka-dot frog? Who can see this flashy glow? Herpetologists haven't found the answers...*yet!*

Do other frogs glow?

Why not add a UV flashlight to your herpetology kit and investigate?

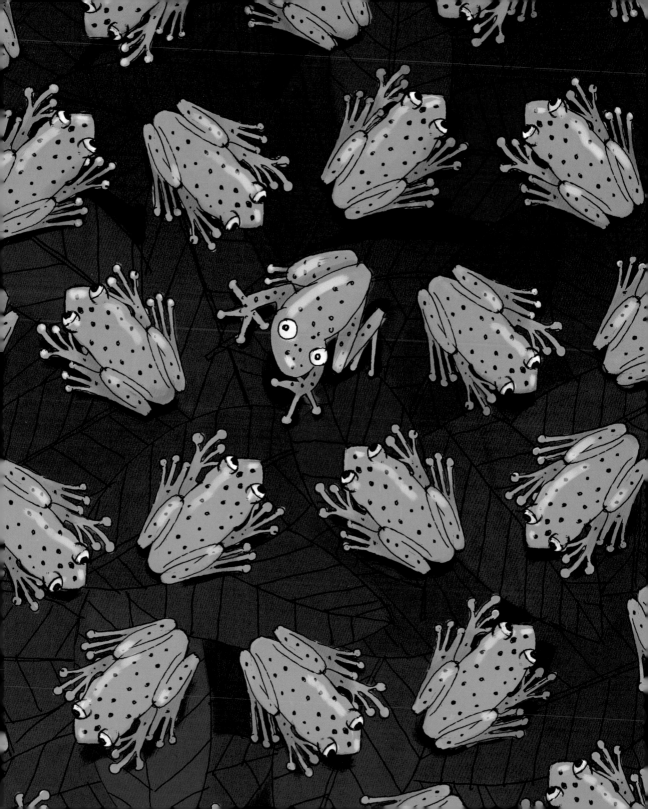

The Speed Eater

While swimming in its grassland pond,
This frog's exceptionally fond,
Of gobbling down its prey, unchewed,
Two hands to mouth, it stuffs in food.

Frog surface-breathes, then scoots beneath.
It lacks a tongue, has no frog teeth.
Frog stirs a cloak of mud. Unviewed,
frog hides inside to ambush food.

Mosquito larva, tadpole, worm,
Quite mushy-dead, or live and firm,
These treats all put frog in the mood
To shove down scads of finger food.

Each hind webbed foot wears three black claws
For tearing larger prey, because
A gape-mouthed gulp would just be *rude*—
Instead, frog shreds, then stuffs in food.

African Clawed Frog

Some frog species lunge at passing prey, then grab and swallow with the help of their short, flat tongues. Large frogs may swallow small rodents or birds. But most frogs flip out long, sticky tongues to snap up prey. And most have upper teeth used to *grip* their meal, not *chew* it.

The African clawed frog (*Xenopus laevis*) has neither tongue nor teeth. But that doesn't stop this gray-green aquatic frog from eating everything it can get its hands on! When it senses underwater vibrations from small prey such as worms, insect larvae, or even tadpoles, it reaches out over and over with long, grabby fingers and quickly stuffs food into its mouth.

Laboratory studies with African clawed frogs have led to improvements in human medical care, but pet frogs released into the wild have often survived and bred, causing problems for native frogs in California and elsewhere in the world.

Active at night, this super swimmer is also a scavenger that eats dead animals. It tears larger carcasses or prey with its sharp hind claws, then furiously shovels in the shreds. Such manners!

Desert Spadefoot Days

down under scorched sand
pudgy toad-spuds dream of
cloudburst nights
tasty termite swarms
mates *whoop-whooping* until dawn

Australian Desert Spadefoot Toad

The Australian desert spadefoot "toad" (*Notaden nichollsi*), which is not a member of the true toad family, must keep its skin moist in its harsh, dry climate. This super-digger uses the tough, spade-shaped part of its hind feet to burrow, back-end-first, deep enough to find moist sand and hide from the sun. The spadefoot toad may surface at night to forage for insects and then retreat back underground again, spending most of its life sharing a narrow burrow with a few other spadefoots or related species. Using another froggy trick to protect thin skin from drying air, they tuck their legs and hunker in the shape of a small, roundish potato.

Following a daytime downpour, Australian desert spadefoot toads stream from their burrows in a nighttime mating throng. Females deposit fertilized eggs in rain puddles. Spadefoot tadpoles hatch and metamorphose quickly (in about a month), hurrying to sprout their own rugged shovel-feet before their birth puddles dry out.

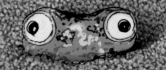

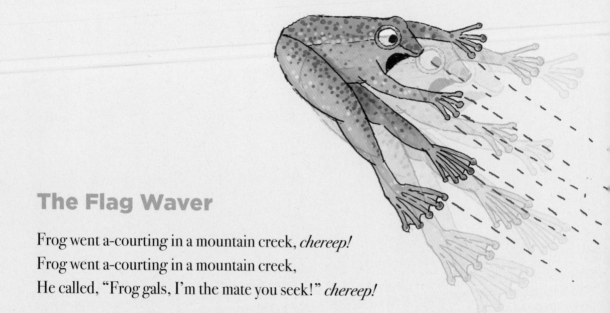

The Flag Waver

Frog went a-courting in a mountain creek, *chereep!*
Frog went a-courting in a mountain creek,
He called, "Frog gals, I'm the mate you seek!" *chereep!*

He perched on a rock and sang his tune, *chereep!*
He perched on a rock and sang his tune,
His vocal sac puffed like a white balloon, *chereep!*

Next, Frog kicked his flag foot high, *boi-oing!*
Next, Frog kicked his flag foot high,
A dance move meant for his lady's eye, *boi-oing!*

A rival hopped up next to him, *boi-oing!*
A rival hopped up next to him,
Frog's foot shot out—*FLAG!*—TAKE A SWIM! *boi-oing!*

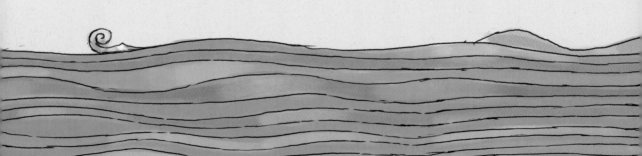

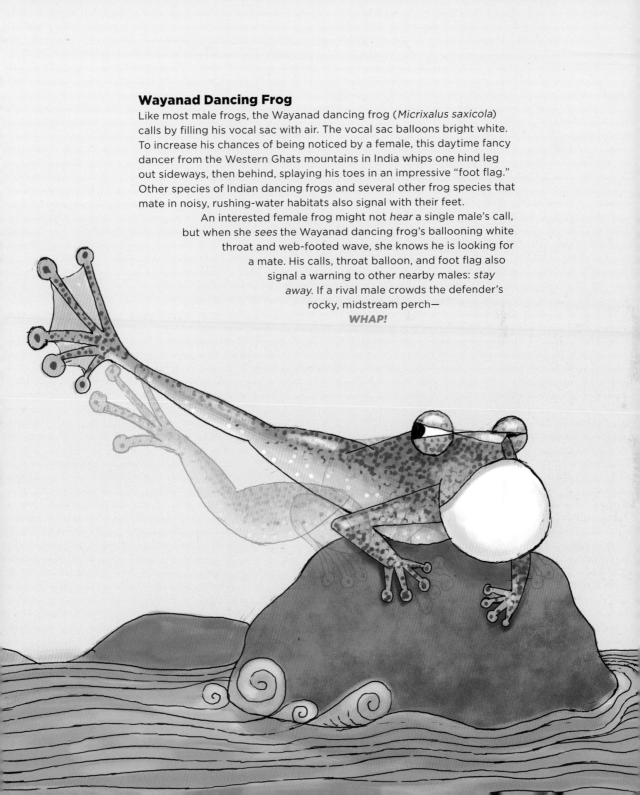

Wayanad Dancing Frog

Like most male frogs, the Wayanad dancing frog (*Micrixalus saxicola*) calls by filling his vocal sac with air. The vocal sac balloons bright white. To increase his chances of being noticed by a female, this daytime fancy dancer from the Western Ghats mountains in India whips one hind leg out sideways, then behind, splaying his toes in an impressive "foot flag." Other species of Indian dancing frogs and several other frog species that mate in noisy, rushing-water habitats also signal with their feet.

An interested female frog might not *hear* a single male's call, but when she *sees* the Wayanad dancing frog's ballooning white throat and web-footed wave, she knows he is looking for a mate. His calls, throat balloon, and foot flag also signal a warning to other nearby males: *stay away.* If a rival male crowds the defender's rocky, midstream perch—
WHAP!

Nothing Up Her Sleeve... PRESTO!

This flat toad can't sit up—she splays
in muddy, sluggish waters, lays eggs
somersaulting with her mate,
their underwater tumbling date
ends with her eggs stuck on her back—
a built-in incubator pack!

Her skin grows pockets, capped with lids,
to shield her embryonic kids,
whose tails shrink as they sprout four legs,
no tadpoles hatch—they stay in eggs,
'til star-shaped toe and pointy snout
poke through Mom's skin...*pop, pop* they're out!

They're huge-mouthed, hungry, seeking prey,
so each toad kid quick-kicks away
from nearby toadlet sis or brother—
hunters who might eat each other.

Star-Fingered Toad

The star-fingered toad (*Pipa pipa*) from South America and Trinidad is a web-footed swimmer that spends most of its life kicking and rowing underwater. Bumpy brown skin and no teeth earn this frog the name star-fingered "toad," but it is not a member of the true toad family.

Hiding in plain sight on a pond or river bottom, this flat frog resembles a dead leaf. It probes the mud with its sensitive fingers to startle up a worm or small fish. Then it opens its mouth wide so water and prey flow in—*GULP!*

Mating star-fingered toads somersault together underwater. Each time around, the female lays several eggs while the male adds his sperm. As they turn, the newly fertilized eggs drop onto the female's back and stick there. The skin on Mama frog's back grows into spongy, covered brood pouches for each of her 60 to 100 eggs. Developing tadpoles stay inside their eggs while they grow legs and absorb their tadpole tails. At hatching time, tiny froglets poke through the brood pouch covers to hop out and start their own ambush predator lives.

The Canopy Climber

This toxic frog, no good to eat,
performs a death-defying feat.
Red as berries, blue-jeans legs,
she helps her tadpoles beat the heat.

When tadpoles hatch on leaves below,
she'll take them froggy-back and go,
away up tree trunks, leaf to leaf,
with tadpoles (one to four) in tow.

She'll reach the canopy; she's spry.
She'll seek small pools that never dry—
bromeliads that cling to trees
and trap rain pockets near the sky.

One tadpole plops in each leaf pool,
where it can grow up, safe and cool.
Frog mama hops on daily rounds,
and drops in pearls of tadpole fuel.

Impatiently each tadpole begs,
for Mama's undeveloped eggs—
the food that turns these tads to frogs
who hop away on blue-jeans legs.

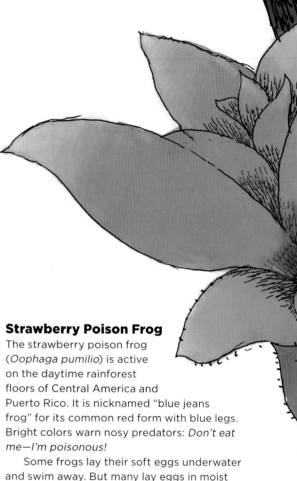

Strawberry Poison Frog

The strawberry poison frog (*Oophaga pumilio*) is active on the daytime rainforest floors of Central America and Puerto Rico. It is nicknamed "blue jeans frog" for its common red form with blue legs. Bright colors warn nosy predators: *Don't eat me—I'm poisonous!*

Some frogs lay their soft eggs underwater and swim away. But many lay eggs in moist spots on land and may stick around to care for eggs, tadpoles, or froglets. The strawberry mom lays her handful of eggs on leaf litter while the dad hangs onto her back to add his sperm in a posture called "amplexus." He'll stay nearby and pee on their eggs to keep them moist until they hatch.

Mom piggybacks her new tadpoles way up into the canopy. She sets each in its own pool of rainwater amid the stout leaves of a clinging bromeliad (bro-MEE-lee-ad) plant. Returning every day or two, she lays unfertilized eggs to feed each stashed tadpole. In six to eight weeks the tadpoles metamorphose into tiny, jumping strawberry poison froglets.

The Frog Swallower

This small warty father,
Nose pointed and slender,
Takes tadpole care further
Than any (frog) other.
With no help from mother,
He guards eggs on litter,
Until larvae quiver
Through jelly-clear covers.

Then trusty Dad gathers
His egg sons and daughters,
And *gulp!* provides shelter,
Where eggs hatch and prosper.
His vocal sac stretching, Dad nurtures, a giver,
'Til tadpoles turn froglets, then *BUUURP*–
Dad delivers!

Darwin's Frog

Frogs make their distinctive chirrups and ribbits by pushing air over their vocal cords. Most frog singers are males advertising to females or claiming a territory. The air in their balloonlike vocal sacs makes their calls much LOUDER.

The male Darwin's frog (*Rhinoderma darwinii*) calls with a quiet *pip-pip-pip-pip* because he uses his large vocal sac for a different task. Most male frogs don't care for young. But a female Darwin's frog lays her eggs and hops away, leaving Dad to stand guard on the daytime forest floors of Chile and Argentina. When tiny developing tadpoles move inside their clear eggs, Dad swallows them into his large vocal sac. The protected eggs hatch in about three days. At first the tadpoles' skin absorbs the frothy, nutritious liquid Dad makes for them in his vocal sac; later the tadpoles can swallow it. In seven to ten weeks, when the tadpoles metamorphose, Dad opens his mouth, and out hop froglets!

The Daredevil Free-Climbers

Some tadpoles wriggle,
they swim and they squiggle,
in puddles or rivers or bogs.

Others hatch mired in muck,
metamorphosing, stuck
wiggle-squirming, 'til they become frogs.

We hatch right away
(in just over a day),
the end of our egg phase comes quick.

Then we scale waterfalls,
doing suction-mouthed crawls,
in our bouldering, free-climbing trick.

Morning, night, afternoon,
through the northeast monsoon,
stuck on stones where cascading rains flow,

We will teethe scummy plants,
then slurp termites and ants
when we're fat burrow frogs, down below!

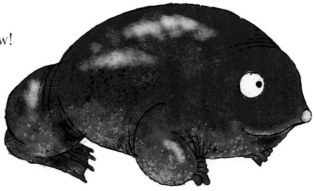

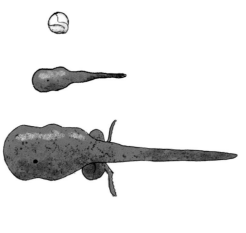

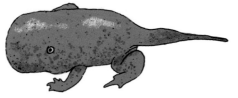

Bhupathy's Purple Frog

Frogs begin life as jellylike eggs, most laid in or near water. Species that hatch as free-living tadpoles mostly scrape underwater surfaces for algae to eat, and some strain tiny plants and dead matter from water. Some tadpoles nibble plants, unhatched frog eggs, and even each other if things get tough in the pond!

Bhupathy's purple frog (*Nasikabatrachus bhupathi*) is a globby, pointy-nosed frog that lives most of its life underground in rocky mountains of southwest India. When monsoon-season rains drench their dry habitat, adult Bhupathy's frogs come up from their burrows, mate, and lay eggs in streambeds flowing with rainwater.

Bhupathy's tadpoles wriggle out of their eggs quickly—in just one to two days. They use their sucker-mouths to squirm up wet rocks against rushing, seasonal cascades. They'll cling there for nearly four months, scraping teeny algae plants from the rocks while they grow limbs, lungs, fat purplish bodies, funny noses, and the tough shovel-feet they'll need to dig their own hideaways from the dry-season heat.

The Balancing Act

Tadpoles leap, then surface-skitter,
Strong tails flip them out of danger.
Hungry fish is bitter, grumbles:
"Am I predator? Or quitter?"
Once they lose those tails...*frog supper!*

Growing tadpoles, long-finned, limber,
Laugh at fish who lurks down under:
"You won't eat us now *or* later!
Leggy? Webbed feet? Even *better*–
When we're frogs we'll *skip* on water!"

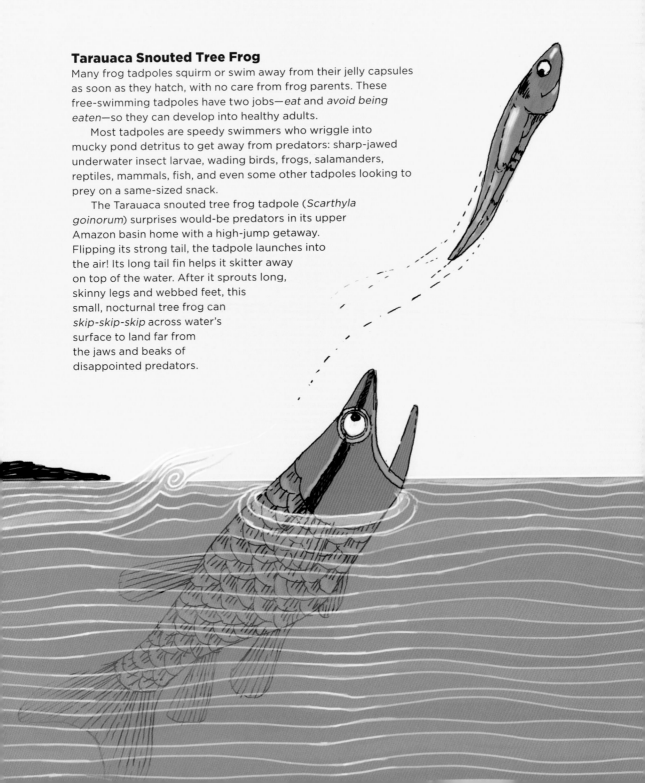

Tarauaca Snouted Tree Frog

Many frog tadpoles squirm or swim away from their jelly capsules as soon as they hatch, with no care from frog parents. These free-swimming tadpoles have two jobs—*eat* and *avoid being eaten*—so they can develop into healthy adults.

Most tadpoles are speedy swimmers who wriggle into mucky pond detritus to get away from predators: sharp-jawed underwater insect larvae, wading birds, frogs, salamanders, reptiles, mammals, fish, and even some other tadpoles looking to prey on a same-sized snack.

The Tarauaca snouted tree frog tadpole (*Scarthyla goinorum*) surprises would-be predators in its upper Amazon basin home with a high-jump getaway. Flipping its strong tail, the tadpole launches into the air! Its long tail fin helps it skitter away on top of the water. After it sprouts long, skinny legs and webbed feet, this small, nocturnal tree frog can *skip-skip-skip* across water's surface to land far from the jaws and beaks of disappointed predators.

The Marathoners

These salamanders make no sound,
They never croak or squeak or squawk,
When sleety rain soaks thawing ground,
They walk and walk and walk and walk.

The puddle where they hatched from eggs,
Glued tight to twig or grassy stalk,
Is where they head on four short legs,
With miles to go, they walk and walk.

Across dark forest, field, and glade,
They join the throng, no need for talk,
No mating call, no serenade,
A wiggle-stepping night parade
Toward home-sweet-pool where water's cool and salamander eggs are laid,
They walk and walk and walk and walk and WALK!

Small-Mouthed Salamander

Adult small-mouthed salamanders (*Ambystoma texanum*) are long-distance walkers that hide under logs and in small soil tunnels by day. Near winter's end, when the first drenching rains fall on their habitats in the central United States and Canada, small-mouthed salamanders travel in a nighttime throng to the vernal pools where they first hatched. Once there, they swim in a silent water ballet, sending chemical messages to attract mates instead of croaking the way frogs do.

Females follow chemical trails to the tiny packets of sperm that males deposit in the pool. They take up the sperm to fertilize the eggs inside their bodies. Females glue their fertilized eggs to leaves and twigs in or near their breeding pool. Eggs hatch, and swimming larvae will metamorphose into walkers before their temporary home puddle dries up in the warming spring.

Other members of this group known as "mole" salamanders also migrate in nighttime marches. But small-mouthed salamanders win the gold for walking 8.7 miles (14 kilometers), farther than any other salamander studied!

The Living Statues

If I can't hide,
or run away,
I spread my four feet out,
I stay.

My bright undersides shout:
Look this way!
My orange danger sign—

No way!
My head's held high,
my tail coils higher,
like a fiddlehead on fire—
I'm deadly poisonous—
You're a liar!

If I can't hide,
or run away,
I spread my four feet out,
I stay.

Say hey!
My waving tail shouts:
Look this way!
An orange danger sign—

I'm not poisonous.
OK. True.
But predators skip *me* thinking I'm *you.*
And I do tricks that you *can't* do:
My tail leaks drops of sticky glue,
and drops off—*hah!*—
still wriggling, too,
then grows right back as good as new.
Though "right back" means a *year...*
or *two...*
sigh.

Rough-Skinned Newt **and**
Yellow-Eyed Ensatina

Most salamanders blend with their surroundings and play statue to hide from predators such as birds, snakes, small mammals, or other salamanders. Salamanders in the group known as newts have deadly toxins in their skins. Newts hide, but also bend into crazy shapes, flashing bright body parts that warn predators *not* to try a bite. Some frogs warn would-be predators this same way.

The **rough-skinned newt** (*Taricha granulosa*) lives on land and breeds in fresh water near the Pacific coast of North America. It has knobbly, brownish skin on its back, but when threatened it arches its chin upward and spirals its tail, showing off bright orangey undersides that warn: *I'm poisonous!*

Among vertebrates, salamanders are tops at regrowing tails, legs, and parts of organs inside their bodies. Most of the family known as "lungless salamanders" can lose their tails *on purpose* to confuse predators and get away. But they can't use this life-saving escape trick often because regrowing a tail costs a lot of energy.

One lungless salamander, the **yellow-eyed ensatina** (*Ensatina eschscholtzii xanthoptica*), shares its Pacific coast habitat with the poisonous, rough-skinned newt. The ensatina's skin oozes sticky, bad-tasting glue, but when it flashes a look-alike orange belly, predators don't know it's only *pretending* to be as deadly as its newty neighbor!

The Wrestlers

stinky
wrinkled logs doze
in cold rivers until
prey swims too close to a giant
SNAP...gulp.

master
wrestlers guard dens
for egg-laying mates, with
sharp-toothed takedowns that make rivals
shove off.

flat-head
dads keep new-hatched,
slow-growing giants safe
from predator munchings—no thanks
to moms!

Japanese Giant Salamander

Most land-dwelling salamanders shoot out long, sticky tongues to snag insects, spiders, worms, and other prey. Aquatic salamanders quickly open their mouths to suction in underwater critters. They also catch unlucky snacks that blunder nearby with a quick sideways *SNAP*.

The Japanese giant salamander (*Andrias japonicus*) is a nocturnal water-dweller that can also walk on land. It grows throughout its entire 30- to 50-year life and can reach five feet (1.5 meters) in length. Its skin has wrinkly folds that make extra surface area to help its giant flat body absorb as much oxygen as it needs from the water of its cold, river-bottom home.

Japanese giant salamander dads don't leave sperm packets for mates. They guard several females in a riverbank den and add sperm after the females lay eggs. Nosy males trying to visit the den will meet the den master's vicious teeth!

Some female salamanders care for their eggs, and others, like these giant moms, lay eggs and swim away. But Japanese giant *dads* stick around for months, fanning the underwater eggs with their giant tails, then protecting the remarkably tiny hatchlings.

The Skin Shredders

Have you ever seen a caecilian?
They're amphibians that look snakily reptilian.
Or something like eels—but mostly tail-less and none have fins,
And some hatchlings' first meals are peeled mama skins.

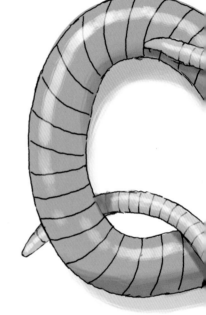

Taita African Caecilian

Caecilians are found in most tropical rainforest habitats. Although smaller species may look like worms, caecilians have backbones. Larger caecilians might be mistaken for snakes but they have thin, moist amphibian skin instead of reptilian scales.

A few caecilians spend their entire lives in fresh water. Most use their hard skulls and strong bodies to tunnel through soil and leaf litter. Tiny tentacles poke in and out of their faces, sensing chemical traces of underwater prey, or of worms, insects, smaller amphibians, or reptiles. Caecilians grab prey with their many short, sharp teeth.

Most caecilians give birth to live young that look a lot like they will as fully developed adults. Some land-dwelling caecilian mamas provide care for their newborns. The Taita African caecilian (*Boulengerula taitana*) from Kenya hatches from its egg and gets right to work chewing outer layers of its mother's specially produced, nutrition-packed skin. With this good start, the hatchling begins growing toward its adult length of about one foot (305 millimeters).

Other caecilians are born fully developed. But before birth those babies scrape nutritious skin from *inside* their mothers with their caecilian baby teeth!

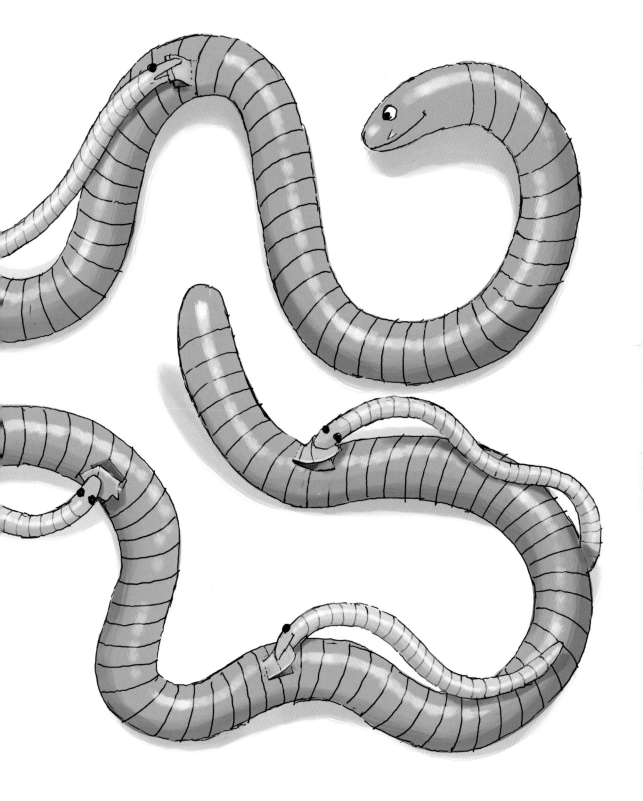

Showstoppers' Farewell

We acrobats have earned a bow. Our show was action-packed!
Now readers, it's *your* turn to try a daring circus act:

Please help protect the habitats on which our lives depend,
It's up to you to keep our wild homes whole and healthy, friend.

We hope you'll take this starring role, more critical each year,
So we can stick to our *best* trick—and POOF, *not* disappear!

Extraordinary and Endangered

Amphibians are found in almost every freshwater and terrestrial (land-based) ecosystem on Earth. They perform important ecosystem jobs, including eating insects and serving as food for other predators.

But habitat loss, diseases spread through international sales of amphibians, and climate change have put five of every ten amphibian species at risk of extinction. They are the most threatened group of organisms on Earth.

To learn what we can do to protect our remarkable amphibian neighbors, please turn to "Amphibians Need Our Help" and check out the resources list on pages 54 and 55. Let's perform our own critically important ecosystem job: serving as the very best stewards we can be of this blue and green planet we all share.

alga—a plant or plantlike organism without roots that lives in salt water or freshwater and uses energy from the sun to make food (two or more are called algae)

ambush predator—a predator that waits for its prey to get close enough to grab without chase or with a very short chase

breeding pool—a small body of water where male and female amphibians mate and produce young

chytridiomycosis (kih-TRID-ee-oh-my-KO-sis)—a potentially deadly amphibian skin infection caused by a "chytrid" (KIH-trid) fungus called *Batrachochytrium dendrobatidis* or "Bd" for short

common name—an animal or plant name in a local language used by people who live in or near its habitat, such as "bullfrog" or "marbled salamander"; an organism can have several different common names

food loop—a two-way food energy connection between organisms in an ecosystem where the young form of one organism (a tadpole, for example) may be preyed upon by another organism (a jumping spider), and that predator (spider) may be eaten by its prey species (frog) in adult form

food web—the many paths food energy takes through organisms such as plants, animals, and microbes feeding on each other in an ecosystem

gland—an organ or group of cells that produces a substance for use elsewhere in the body or for elimination from the body of an animal

invasive species—a non-native animal or plant that reproduces and spreads without natural predators and outcompetes native species for food or habitat

Latin name—the unique, two-part scientific classification name given to every living organism on Earth expressed in this form: *Genus species*; as new discoveries are made, scientific names may change

monsoon—a seasonal wind bringing heavy rains

poetic license—making up words, breaking rules of grammar and poetic form for a particular poetic effect such as humor, rhythm, or rhyme

poison—a substance that is harmful when ingested (eaten or drunk)

toxin—a harmful, irritating, or bad-tasting substance

ultraviolet light—electromagnetic radiation with wavelengths too short to be visible to the human eye

venom—a harmful substance made by an animal that can be forcibly delivered through the outer covering of another animal

vernal pool—a temporary, seasonal body of water created by rains and/or snowmelt that will reduce in size or dry up during drier seasons

vocal sac—the loose, thin-skinned pouch on the floor or side of a male frog's mouth that can be filled with air to make its call louder

Amphibian Acrobats

"Amphibian Acrobats" has six *stanzas*, or sets of lines. Each stanza has four lines, though the third line in the last stanza is broken into three parts to help slo-o-ow the reader down. The first three lines in each stanza **end rhyme** with each other, and have four STRONG beats:

> WE'RE amPHIbians! We BREATHE through our **SKIN**,
> We DRINK the same WAY: we SOAK water **IN**,
> Through SKIN that is MOIST-ily MARvelous **THIN**—

The last line in each stanza is a *refrain*—a line or part of a line that is repeated. These final lines each have three beats:

> Come SEE our aMAzing *SHOW!*
> All EXcellent SPOTS for our *SHOW!*

The Olympic Jumpers

The first, second, and fifth lines of "The Olympic Jumpers" rhyme, and have three STRONG beats each:

> Some FIji frogs—GOLD with brown TRACes,

In the third line, the word **midair** rhymes with **where** at the beginning of the fifth line. This poem has a rollicking rhythm, mostly alternating a STRONG syllable (part of a word) with two soft syllables, similar to the rhythm in a five-line poem form called a *limerick*.

The Skydiver

This poem is written in three-line stanzas of *cumulating verse*. Cumulating means "adding to." In cumulating verse, we add a consonant sound to the beginning of each line's end-rhyme word. At the end of the first line, the **ar** sound in the word **are** will gain a **t** sound to become **t+ar=tar** at the end of the second line. In the third line, **tar** gains an **s** to become **star**. The second stanza's cumulating verse adds a consonant sound to each line's end-rhyme sound: **eyes**, then **lies**, then **flies**.

The Shape Shifter

A *concrete* or *shape poem* uses the arrangement of words on the page in a certain form to give information about the poem's subject. "The Shape Shifter" takes the form of the pebble toad when the toad is taking the form of a pebble! The poem's loose rhyme scheme uses a partial rhyme called *consonant rhyme*, matching consonant sound **bl** or sometimes **bls** heard at the ends of words like trou**ble**, tum**bles,** or bram**bles**. The **d** sound from the first and last lines also match, leaving a secret message: toa**d**/ungobble**d**.

The Knife Heads

A *dactyl* is a three-part beat with the rhythm STRONG/soft/soft. "The Knife Heads" is a *double dactyl*—an eight-line poem in two stanzas that uses the dactyl rhythm. The first line of a double dactyl always has two nonsense words, each a STRONG/soft/soft beat:

JABB/i/ty STABB/i/ty

Lines two and three also have two STRONG/soft/soft beats. The fourth line in each stanza has one STRONG/soft/soft beat and one STRONG beat at the end:

PRE/da/tors CROAK!

For extra challenge, the second line in the first stanza is the name of a person or place, and the second line in the last stanza should be one long, six-syllable word that has a STRONG/soft/soft/STRONG/soft/soft rhythm. *Whew!*

The Deep-Freeze Artist

"The Deep-Freeze Artist" is a *triolet*—an eight-line poem with just two rhyme sounds. In this poem the rhyme sounds are **frost** and **freeze**. The rhyme scheme is ABaAabAB. This notation is like a code with one letter standing in for each line. Lines given the same letter (such as A and a) rhyme with each other. The two lines are exact repeats if their letters are the same *and* capitalized (A and A). So the first, fourth, and seventh lines are repeats that rhyme with lines three and five, and the second and eighth lines are repeats that rhyme with line six.

The Flash!

"The Flash!" is written in *Skeltonic verse*, a form that uses short lines and lots of rhyme with no set pattern, and any number of stanzas. Here I've used just one rhyme sound springing from "glows," but Skeltonic verse can have many rhyming sounds.

The Speed Eater

"The Speed Eater" is a *kyrielle*. This poem form is written in four-line stanzas. The first two lines in each stanza rhyme with each other, forming a *rhyming couplet*. The third and fourth lines in each stanza also rhyme with each other. The fourth line in each stanza (or the end of the fourth line in each stanza, as in this poem) is repeated. The challenge is to find enough rhyming words to repeat the end rhyme sound in *all* of the poem's stanzas! In this poem I've rhymed **food** with **unchewed**, **unviewed**, **mood**, and finally, **rude**.

Desert Spadefoot Days

"Desert Spadefoot Days" is a *tanka*—an ancient, five-line Japanese poem form. In Japanese, the number of syllables in each of the tanka's five lines should be 5, 7, 5, 7, 7 (31 in all). English language tanka poets use five short lines to paint the images they want to share, keeping the total to fewer than 31 syllables in all, without as strict a line count. The third line of a tanka (in this poem: "cloudburst nights") may be viewed as a turning point between two short poems: lines 1–3 can be read as the first poem, and lines 3–5 as the second poem.

The Flag Waver

Poems we already know can give us form, rhythm, and a pattern to follow when we write our own new poems. *Song lyrics* are poems with built-in music—rhythm and rhyme patterns we can use to create our own new version. "The Flag Waver" follows the rhythm and rhyme scheme in one version of an old American folk song, "Froggie Went A-Courting."

Nothing Up Her Sleeve… PRESTO!

Each line in this poem has four STRONG beats:

> This FLAT toad CAN'T sit UP—she SPLAYS

The poem also uses a poetic element called *enjambment*, which means an idea doesn't end at the end of a line, but continues into the middle of the next line. If I were to separate the first stanza into ideas instead of into four-beat sections it might look like this:

> This flat toad can't sit up.
> She splays in muddy, sluggish waters.
> Lays eggs, somersaulting with her mate.
> Their underwater tumbling date ends with her eggs stuck on her back—
> A built-in incubator pack.

But I chose to follow the beats instead of the ideas because I'm using one of my most favorite poetic elements: *poetic license!*

The Canopy Climber

Persian is the official language of Iran. The *ruba'i* is an ancient Persian stanza form with four lines, in which three of the lines—the first, second, and fourth—all rhyme. "The Canopy Climber" is a *rubaiyat*—a poem written with more than one ruba'i stanza. Just for fun, I hopped the one nonrhyming sound from the first stanza down to the last stanza to use as the rhyme sound there: **legs**.

The Frog Swallower

"The Frog Swallower" is written with short lines ending in *partial rhyme*. Each ending word finishes with the soft sound -**er** as in FATH**er**, SLEND**er**, FURTH**er**. But the STRONG syllables don't match, so these end words are not *perfect rhymes*. There is one perfect end-rhyme pair—can you hear it? BROTH**er** would rhyme with those two end-rhyme words *perfectly!*

The Daredevil Free-Climbers

This poem has six stanzas with three short lines in each. It could also be written in three longer stanzas with the first stanza looking like this:

> Some tadpoles wriggle, they swim and they squiggle,
> in puddles or rivers or bogs.
> Others hatch mired in mud, metamorphosing, stuck
> wiggle-squirming, 'til they become frogs.

In this form the poem is a *common measure* or a *ballad stanza*, a form with four lines per stanza in an alternating rhythm of four beats, three beats, four beats, three beats. In the ballad stanza, the second and fourth lines rhyme with each other. The first and third lines may also rhyme with each other.

The Balancing Act

The word "skitter" inspired the rhymes in "The Balancing Act," a free-rhyming poem that has no form or set number of lines. Two words are perfect rhymes: **bitter** and **quitter**. Other words, such as **skip** and **finned** share the short **i** sound with **skitter**. All of the *partial end rhymes*, such as **limber**, **water**, and **better**, end with the **er** sound—all except one. Can you find it? Here's a hint: that end word shares the **uh** sound with the words **under** and **supper**.

The Marathoners

The four-beat rhythm in "The Marathoners" was inspired by the determined, four-legged pace of these migrating salamanders. The poem was built around the line:

> They walk and walk and walk and walk.

This line is repeated (with some changes) at the end of each of the three stanzas. The final stanza adds some lines to build the excitement, play with more rhyme, and make room for an extra WALK!

The Living Statues

This is a *poem for two voices* with lots of rhyme, best enjoyed aloud with two readers. Each reader takes one "part"—either the **newt** or the ensatina. In this poem both critters begin together, speaking the same lines in unison. That's why the first four lines in both columns line up exactly. Next the **newt** speaks, and then the ensatina follows, saying *almost* the same words...but not quite. Why? How do *italics* change the way you read the *italicized* words in a poem or sentence?

The Wrestlers

"The Wrestlers" is a *cinquain* (SINK-ane), a five-line, syllable-counting poem form developed by Adelaide Crapsey, an American poet who studied Japanese poem forms. Cinquain poems follow this pattern: two syllables, four, six, eight, two. Since I've used three linked cinquain stanzas, I'll call this poem a "linquain"!

The Skin Shredders

This is a *clerihew*—a funny four-line poem about someone, written in two rhyming couplets. The lines in a clerihew can be any number of STRONG beats or syllables, and the number of STRONG beats do not have to match. But a clerihew still has rules! The first line introduces the name of the person, and the second line has to rhyme with the name. The third and fourth lines rhyme with each other, and they tell something more about that person. My "person" is the caecilian!

Showstoppers' Farewell

This last poem is a series of three rhyming couplets. Each line has seven STRONG beats: We ACroBATS have EARNED a BOW. Our SHOW was ACtion-PACKED!

While researching this book, I had the tremendous luck to leap onto a "Save the Frogs" ecotour with a knowledgeable group of herpetology enthusiasts in a hands-on amphibian learning adventure. Huge thanks to Dr. Kerry Kriger (*www.savethefrogs.com*) and Michael Starkey (*www.savethesnakes.org*) for inviting me on the tour and agreeing to review the completed manuscript. I am ever grateful for the generosity of spirit shared with this neophyte "herper" by every tour member and by our guide, Carlos Roberto Chavarria.

I am thankful that reading about the migration of small-mouthed salamanders led me to Dr. Robert Denton, who was happy to answer questions, then marched on to review the entire manuscript. Dr. William Duellman was kind to answer my query concerning the Tarauaca snouted tree frog, and Dr. Jodi Rowley took a moment from her exciting Australian FROGID app project to discuss the Australian desert spadefoot toad. A question about Bhupathy's purple frog led me to Dr. Elizabeth Prendini, whose interest and enthusiasm for science communication resulted in her generous review of the entire manuscript. I am also grateful to friend and brilliant art cartographer Connie Brown for her input regarding map projections.

Unending thanks to my pond of joyful support, including writers Doe Boyle, Mary-Kelly Busch (thank you for Save the Frogs, MK!), Leslie Connor, Lorraine Jay, Kay Kudlinski, Judy Theise, and Nancy Elizabeth Wallace; everyone at Peachtree Publishing Company Inc.; my beloved family; and the nonstop, hop-on-it creativity of illustrator Robert Meganck.

And finally, I would also like to express my gratitude to the CT State Department of Economic and Community Development for awarding me the Artist Fellowship that supported this project.

–L. B.

Amphibians are found in almost every freshwater and terrestrial ecosystem on Earth, but most species need particular temperature and moisture conditions to survive. When forests and open spaces are cleared for human use, amphibians lose their habitats. None of them can travel very far, nor can they easily skip over developed areas in search of a more hospitable neighborhood.

International sale of wild amphibians for pets, food, and medicines also impacts their survival. Imported amphibians can infect local populations with serious diseases such as chytridiomycosis or may become invasive. Home populations of exported amphibians decline and their ecosystems suffer while insect pests they would have eaten multiply.

Changing climate impacts amphibians, too. Climate stress can weaken their bodies' natural defenses against diseases. Climate change–induced droughts can leave their ponds dry at the wrong time, with terrible consequences for reproduction. New species of amphibians are being discovered each year, but our planet is also losing amphibians at an alarming rate.

Fortunately, there are many ways to help! We can make sure our yards, parks, wetlands, and open spaces provide pesticide and herbicide-free, healthy habitat for local amphibians. We can support organizations working to restore and reconnect amphibian habitat elsewhere. We can pass laws to ban the international trade of wild amphibians. We can educate ourselves and work locally and globally to reduce the effects of climate change. And we can study these fascinating animals in zoos and in the wild so they can teach us the best ways to help!

Get Your Boots Wet!

Local chapters of nature associations such as your state's Audubon Society often host amphibian hikes. Try an online search with your state name, "frog," and "hike" in the search box. A herpetologist at your local college or university may be glad to share their research adventures with your class. You can even become a citizen scientist and help monitor amphibians in your area by joining your local chapter of Frogwatch USA at *www.aza.org/frogwatch-usa-chapter-list.*

Resources

AmphibiaWeb 2019. *www.amphibiaweb.org*. University of California, Berkeley, CA, USA. Accessed 3 July 2019. A one-stop portal for general, educational, and conservation information and a worldwide amphibian database.

Attenborough, Sir David. *Life in Cold Blood*. BBC (2008). *www.bbc.co.uk/programmes/b008yvv2*. This five-episode field documentary explores Earth's incredible amphibians and reptiles.

Bates, Mary. "The Creature Feature: 10 Fun Facts about Caecilians." *Wired*, November 4, 2013, *www.wired.com/2013/11/the-creature-feature-10-fun-facts-about-caecilians-or-this-amphibian-is-one-in-a-caecilian*. This overview of caecilians includes a video of young caecilians feeding on their mama's skin!

IUCN 2018. *The IUCN Red List of Threatened Species*. Version 2019-2. *www.iucnredlist.org*. Downloaded on 29 April 2019. This reference is the source of our range map and species' vulnerability data.

Naish, Darren. "The Amazing World of Salamanders." *Tetrapod Zoology* (blog), *Scientific American*, October 1, 2013, *blogs.scientificamerican.com/tetrapod-zoology/the-amazing-world-of-salamanders*. Natural history of salamanders with scientific illustration and photos.

Amphibian Rescue Organizations

EDGE: Top 100 EDGE Amphibians. *www.edgeofexistence.org/species/species-category/amphibians*. Supports worldwide conservation projects for critically endangered species.

Save the Frogs. *www.savethefrogs.com*. Supports amphibian education and habitat restoration worldwide and provides hands-on learning for eco-travelers.

Captive Breeding Conservation Programs

Amphibian Ark: Keeping Threatened Amphibian Species Afloat. *www.amphibianark.org/education/what-are-amphibians*

Smithsonian's National Zoo Conservation and Biology Institute. *nationalzoo.si.edu/center-for-species-survival/amphibians*

How Many Known Amphibian Species?

frogs and toads	7098
salamanders	731
caecilians	212
all amphibians	8041

At least 170 known amphibian species are presumed to have gone extinct.

Used with the permission of AmphibiaWeb, accessed on 3 July 2019

Used with the permission of IUCN Red List, accessed on 21 April 2019

Where Do Amphibian Acrobats Live?

The habitat ranges of our Amphibian Acrobat species are shown on this map in the color of each critter's circular icon. Worldwide, amphibians are found on every continent except Antartica.

rough-skinned newt

yellow-eyed ensatina

African clawed frog*

strawberry poison frog

star-fingered toad

Tarauaca snouted tree frog

African clawed frog*

Darwin's frog

North American wood frog

small-mouthed salamander

Venezuelan pebble toad

Greening's frog

polka-dot tree frog

Bruno's casque-headed frog

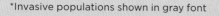

*Invasive populations shown in gray font

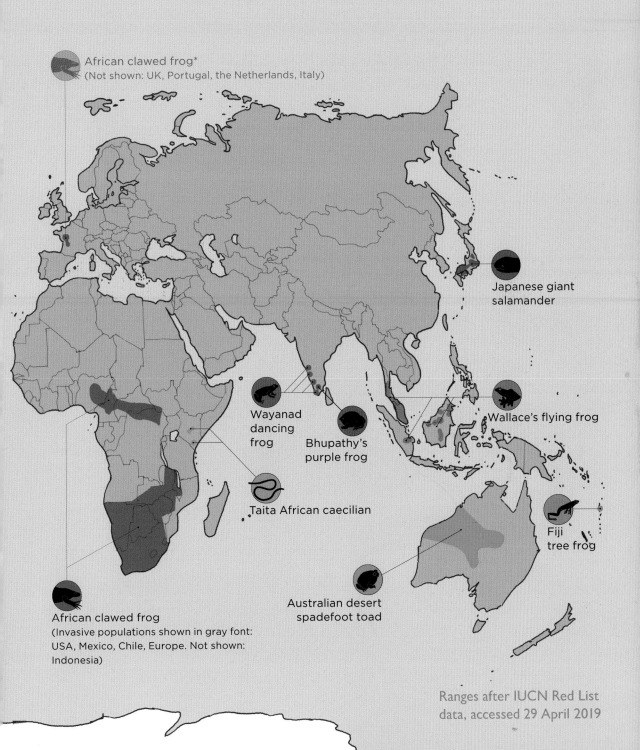

African clawed frog*
(Not shown: UK, Portugal, the Netherlands, Italy)

Japanese giant
salamander

Wayanad
dancing
frog

Bhupathy's
purple frog

Wallace's flying frog

Taita African caecilian

Fiji
tree frog

Australian desert
spadefoot toad

African clawed frog
(Invasive populations shown in gray font:
USA, Mexico, Chile, Europe. Not shown:
Indonesia)

Ranges after IUCN Red List
data, accessed 29 April 2019

Venezuelan pebble toad

strawberry poison frog

US nickel

Tarauaca snouted tree frog

Darwin's frog

polka-dot tree frog

Wayanad dancing frog

Bhupathy's purple frog*

Fiji tree frog

Australian desert spadefoot toad

I'm of Least Concern for now, but like many others, my numbers are decreasing.

Bruno's casque-headed frog

North American wood frog

Greening's frog

star-fingered toad

My population is decreasing, too.

Wallace's flying frog

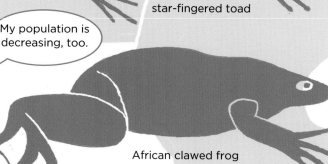

African clawed frog

Amphibian Acrobats: Relative Sizes and Threat of Extinction

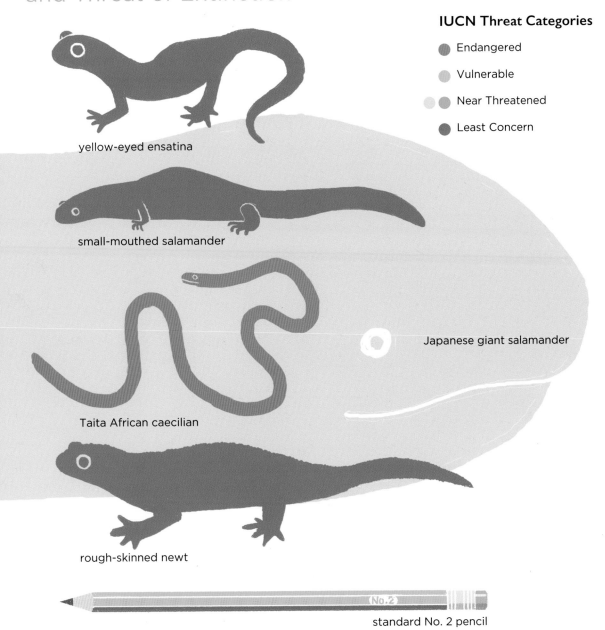

IUCN Threat Categories

- Endangered
- Vulnerable
- Near Threatened
- Least Concern

yellow-eyed ensatina

small-mouthed salamander

Japanese giant salamander

Taita African caecilian

rough-skinned newt

standard No. 2 pencil

*Identified in one location only and believed to be endangered, as is its closest relative, the Indian purple frog (*Nasikabatrachus sahyadrensis*).

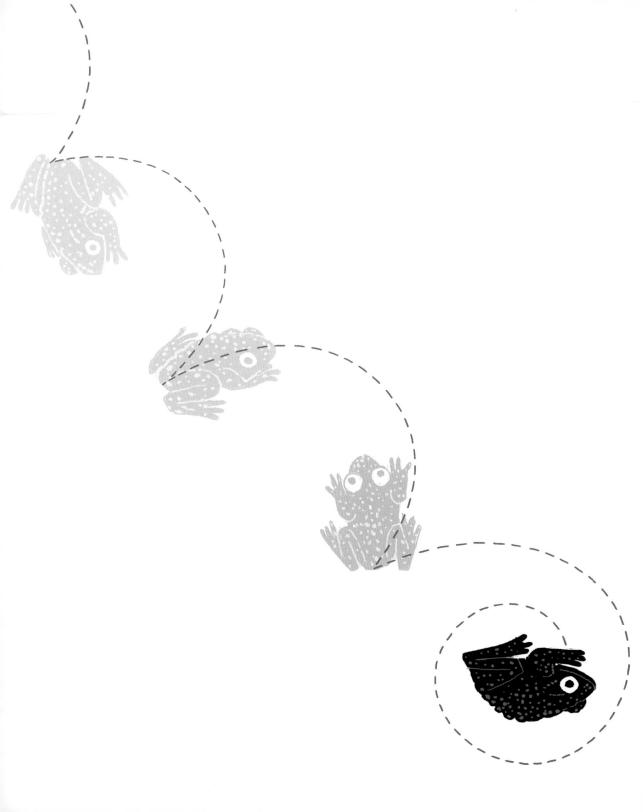

Tarauaca snouted tree frog

Greening's frog

Wallace's flying frog

Darwin's frog

Australian desert spadefoot toad

yellow-eyed ensatina

African clawed frog

strawberry poison frog

Venezuelan pebble toad

small-mouthed salamander

star-fingered toad

Taita African caecilian